DANCING THE WAVES
and OTHER POEMS

STEVEN CURRY

for Donna
My Partner in the Waves

Dancing the Waves and Other Poems
by Steven Curry

printed in Thailand

Published by Anoai Press 1998

ISBN 0-9653971-5-7

cover photograph
Mark Cunningham riding underwater at
Half Point, Sandy Beach, O'ahu, 1995.
Photographer: Wayne Levin

backcover photo: Ted Padres

distributed by
Anoai Press
3349-A Anoai Place
Honolulu, Hawaii 96822
USA
Phone (808) 988-6109
internet 75032.1403@CompuServe.com

first printing 1998

Acknowledgements

Many thanks to Wayne Levin for permission to use his
photographs from *Through a Liquid Mirror*,
an Editions Limited Book. I am grateful for his patience
and kindness in helping me make certain selections. At the
same time I should thank Mark Cunningham for allowing
me to use the photograph of him for my cover.
I am grateful, also, to Coleman Barks for permission
to use the translations of the poems of Rumi that he
and John Moyne have published through Maypop,
Threshold Books, and Copper Beech Press.
And, again, I am indebted to Frank Stewart for his kind
and perceptive words about my work.

The Ocean has an eye.

. . . .
We should wake up and look with the clear Eye
of the water we float upon.

—Rumi

Always add the gratitude clause
to any sentence, If God Wills,
then go.

—Rumi

Contents

INSTRUCTIONS FOR A BEGINNING SURFER

> Listen to presences inside poems.
> Let them take you where they will.
>
> Follow those private hints,
> And never leave the premises.
> —Rumi

Do not swim where the beach is steep
or where channels cut through the reef.
Do not swim in murky water
or near the mouth of a river.
In fact, if you cannot swim,
do not go into the water at all.

Sometimes the water tugs at your board,
pulls it backward, draws it down
where the waves hollow out as the undertow
drains through a channel in the reef.
Or it just may be the hungry ghost of a man
or a woman lost at sea reaching out
for someone to keep it company.

Do not sleep in the room of a house
where tree branches touch the roof.
Always step across a threshold quickly
and never linger in front of a open door.
Never stare directly at a movement
caught out of the corner of your eye.
Never look back when leaving a graveyard,
and never turn your back on the sea.

WAVES AT EVENING (Summer)

Being is not what it seems,
nor non-being. The world's
existence is not
in the world.
                    —Rumi

Just after sunset frigate birds
like something prehistoric
Come in from sea, riding the high
thermals and the dark-blue sky,
Across the face of the crescent moon.

I turn the longboard toward shore—paddle
into the dark-blue hollow
of the wave, tuck myself in, to ride
Across the crescent face of evening.

"Just to be held by the Ocean
is the best luck we could have."

LATE SESSIONS: WAIKIKI

> . . . creation usually unfolds,
> like calm breakers.
>
> The Ocean has an eye . . . ;
> we should try to wake up
> and look with the clear Eye
> of the water we float upon.
> —Rumi

I

Sometimes when you paddle out to catch a last wave
at evening, still winds and fading light blend
Ocean and sky into a single gray-blue screen—

lines blur, the horizon disappears, and ground swells
approaching from the open sea arrive
like phantoms. You cannot see them until they are
upon you—other times you only glimpse
a faint movement out of the corner of your eye—
if you see them at all. Often it can
be unnerving. To catch a building wave, you have
to be at the solitary place where
the swell jacks up and crests over the reef—a place
hard to find in a landscape where reference
points have vanished—in a weird light, neatly erased.

II

The deceptive wait for a wave is like
drifting in dream-time—disorienting,
but unmistakably real. Here, even
the way-finding of navigators on
voyaging canoes seems a familiar art.
The symbolic becomes real, reality
a terrible disturbance of reason.

As in most things, we blind ourselves because
we look too hard to find the familiar.
When you feel the water begin to sink,
and the ocean pull itself back, gather
itself up, then it's time to find the spot
and swing your board toward shore, paddling to match
speed with that of a wave you only feel.

III

Like one gliding through the thickness of sleep, you haul
yourself across a drowsy borderland between
the anxiety of waking and the comfort
of a dream, waiting to be caught by the heavy
roll of ocean toward shore, the pale grey stretch of sand—
the one line you imagine you still can see. Just
as the wave takes you, the thought occurs, "In water,"
The mystic Rumi says, "all lines are illusions."
Then comes surrender and the willing letting go.

Riding a longboard through evening's dimmly glazed light
is like this: you cross under the liquid shadow
of the wave's crest and awaken with a clear eye—
then still the heart and take the drop into the curl
for the slide across creation's unfolding calm.

DARK RAINBOW

An invisible bird flies over,
but casts a quick shadow.
                        —Rumi

Tonight, just past twilight as the moon rose
from behind the mountain, rain showers blew down
out of the valley obscuring the moon
for a moment before the trades carried
them out to sea. When the squall finally passed,
the reflected light of the moon in mist
folded a ghost-like arc of ashen light
in a dark rainbow over the water.

And where the muted glow touched the ocean
a careful eye could just discern the washed-
out yet clear colors of the full spectrum
asserting themselves against the deepening night.
Bright shards of daylight resist becoming
the past, dissolve in the waves of evening.

SOUTH SHORE, O'AHU

> It's true, then. If the Ocean were not
> in love, it would come to rest somewhere.
> —Rumi

After midnight, as you settle toward sleep,
On full moon nights when a south
wind rides in just ahead of a rising
tide, the surge from the open sea
meets resistance on the shallows a mile out,
pulls back on itself, lifts and courses
across the living surface of the reef,
its coral- and lava-throated voice
echoing from the cliffs of Diamond Head.

Like a face in a mirror, the reflection
tells little, but mountain and ocean
speak secrets in unison: "The sea's many
bright and dark strands are veins. . . .
Your hidden self is blood in those,
those veins that are lute strings that make
ocean music, not the sad edge of surf,
but the sound of no shore." Swim through
your sleep, "all parts of the world are in love."

TOTAL ECLIPSE AT MOONRISE

> No wonder I go mad and disappear for
> three days every month with the moon.
> —Rumi

Looking like a magenta ball cradled
in the raised claw of a Chinese dragon,
The full moon rose tonight out of Diamond
Head crater and hid in the earth's dark red shadow,
Before clouds covered it and rain fell until dawn.

Perhaps tomorrow night the moon won't rise.
Tonight we felt it, though, in the deep roll
Of the ground-swell that steamed in from the south.
All night we knew the pulse of the darkening moon,
Felt the water's movement, heard thunder in the dark.

EVENING GLASS

Your spirit needs to follow
the changes happening in the
spacious place it knows about.
—Rumi

Again the moon rose full and red
over the rim of Diamond Head—
there was no eclipse this time, just
volcanic haze blown up, they say,
from the Big Island to the South.

During the day our eyes water
and burn, our throats are raw, but in
the relief of evening, sunset
and moonrise awe. Even the winds

blow light, variable, barely
a low whisper out of the South.
But whatever surf arrives rolls
in clean, undulant, like scalloped,

tinted crystal—at first a dark
rising swell, then a shimmering wave
rising as it gains mass before
shattering against evening's calm,
splinters of deep, moon tinted glass.

"Bodysurfers"

"SURFING SERIES I"
(after Wayne Levin)

> Words let water from an unseen,
> infinite ocean
> Come into this place as energy for
> the dying and even the dead.
> —Rumi

As if across an overcast sky the surfers glide
through clouds of air and foam under the weight of oceans,
beneath an avalanche of water, collapsing waves,
swept thousands of dark miles by storms in the open sea.

They swim, looking for all the world like gargoyles,
suspended in motion, flying warriors caught by the camera's eye
in still-life, still on patrol, remnants of some mythic army
fighting the war of heaven, still light from a long dead star.

BODYSURFING MAKAPU'U

> Don't insist on going where you
> think you want to go.
> *Ask* the way to the Spring.
> —Rumi

The fist of the wave can snap your back
when it slams you down, knuckles and heel of palm,
and pins you on stone-hard water or sandy bottom.

The bone-jarring shock along your spine
and the crush of water on your chest steals
your breath and your illusions of your own strength.

Up is down—or maybe not. Memories of
sunlight and friends on the beach disappear
as you flail through gritty darkness scratching for air.

Or,

You can cradle yourself in the soft
curl of fingers closing. The ocean's roll:
hollow of fingertips touching the face of the wave's palm.

Riding high in the pocket, blue-green
wonder, the wave's moment holds you up, hurls
you side-slipping as if through grace across its shining face,

Then releases you, rolls you out
beneath it with a soft gesture toward shore
or turns you to ride back to the safety of deep water.

"Underwater Takeoff"

HOW TO ENTER A WAVE

> You engrave this physical image
> everywhere as a sign you've forgotten
> where you're from.
> —Rumi

There are two ways to enter a wave: one
is to wait crouched down beneath the surface,
then to kick as the water lifts you and to push
yourself through the face of the passing swell —
to enter with an assertiveness that
pretends to match strength and agility with the
pull of planets and the sad edge of ages;

the other way is to coil low, washed by
the sea's motion—to insinuate yourself
into the approaching wave, roll into
the curl ahead of the crest, turn and drop,
to be absorbed into the form and force
while remaining separate the way some great poets
insinuate themselves into history's pages.

The ride is like a brief coming to terms
with life, when you become one with it, but
know that your presence is temporary
and unnecessary as you glide and
roll, dancing in the deep hollow of a
wave that is and was and always will be.

MAKAPU'U SHOREBREAK

When you do things from your soul,
you feel a river moving in you, a joy.
—Rumi

Without an outside reef to slow its run
a wave from the open sea rushes the steep
beach fast and hard. When the backwash
of the outgoing swell meets it, the force throws
the wave up into a wall, with a crack as clear
and sharp as thunder. Its own momentum folds it over
into a magnificient but back-breaking barrel
that holds up just long enough to allow a single rider—
suspended in the steep curve, planing on hip and shoulder,
arms extended like a flying angel carves a banking arc,
one palm earthward, the other toward heaven—
to hurl unscathed through slaughter.

To ride this wave you must be in just the right place
and, with yourself and with the unpredictable sea,
have found grace and made an unreasoning peace.

SMALL-DAY WAVE-PLAY

> This singing-art is sea foam.
> The graceful movements come from a pearl
> somewhere on the ocean floor.
>
> Weary of form, I come into Qualities.
> Each Quality says, "I am a blue-green sea.
> Dive into me."
>   —Rumi

There is no way to describe the crystalline water
On a sunlit Makapu'u morning—

how bits of black lava and white buttons
of coral like scattered pillows punctuate
the undulant beige of the sandy bottom;

how the small swell sweeps in, almost invisibly,
in neat lines, as if guided by some unremarkable design
and form waves that fold over into flawless tubes;

how the water itself can be, at once, the white
of sea foam , the blue-green of the Pacific,
and still be as clear as a glass of spring water.

There is no way to describe the crystalline feeling
that comes over you as you coil in the shallows and wait
for the wave that, with a snap-kick and a turn, you will enter—

how you will hang far back in the curl, insinuate yourself
into the wave, and slide through the hollow untouched
like one thrice-blessed slides through privileged moments;

how you are at once ancient and unborn, for a moment
eternal, side-slipping like one forever guiltless
through immediate blue-green clarity and bliss.

IT'S ALL IN WHO YOU KNOW. . . .

> Water, stories, the body,
> all the things we do, are mediums
> that hide and show what's hidden.
> —Rumi

I didn't believe it at first. No one does. But there was no
mistaking something was going on. He said his brother was
a fisherman who had been killed when he fell from the rocks
at Bamboo Ridge. He said, actually, his brother didn't fall—he was
pushed—but it was a case of mistaken identity. He said his brother
had been pushed by ghosts. Ghosts don't usually make mistakes,
but in this case they had, so now they were in his debt—in other words,
they owed him big time. This doesn't make the story any easier to
understand. But the fact remains, when he cupped his hands
together and whumped them on the water and then began
that chant of his, by God, the waves came—big ones too, even
on the the flattest days. True story, you know.

ROGUE WAVES

> . . . but the hurricane of experience
> lashed me out of hiding and made me
>
> a wave moving into shore, saying loudly
> the ocean's secret as I went. . . .
> —Rumi

After a storm, or sometimes before, sets
of rogue waves come in from the open sea,
or sometimes, of course, they don't come at all.

To get caught in the middle of the break
is to get caught in a rip with nowhere
to go—except into the after-life.

Just to stay in one place takes all your strength
and that, in itself, can be fatal. You
can always try to paddle out, to catch

one last wave before surrendering to
the force of the sea. Or you can just turn
your board toward shore and hold on like a dream,

then let the boiling white water launch you
over reef and rip, then, with luck, between
rocks, to dump you stunned but wiser on shore.

CLOSE-OUT SETS: MAKAPU'U
(after Wayne Levin)

> You are so weak. Give up to Grace.
> . . . .
> You need more help than you know.
> —Rumi

When, like most of life's unwelcome trials,
long sets of large, rogue waves sweep in
out of the north-east without a warning,
bodysurfers out in the middle break
are left with nowhere to go except down.
Long sets of eight-foot waves break all the way
across Makapu'u's wide mouth, closing off
retreat toward either land or open sea.

Seconds before the first wave hits, I pause,
then hold my breath, then dive beneath shadows
cast by clouds of water, collapsing waves
folding sea and air into plumes of dark
downward force. I pull against heavy clouds
or flail within an insubstantial haze
of white, looking for the gray channel back
toward ambiguous breath and cloudless sky.

Whimsey says, "Move like a dolphin moves."
I surface, breathe and dive again before
the next wave breaks and pulls me down too hard.
With each wave, I dive less deep than before,
fear the umbilical of Will may break;
fatigue will win, and the last dive will come,
followed by the letting go. I surface
breathe and dive, but this time I know the calm
is coming. No longer stalled "betwixt and between,"
I float toward the threshold and the long sprint
for shore just ahead of the next large set,
humbly grateful for this moment of grace.

"Floating"

PARADISE IN MOONLIGHT

> We are the night ocean filled
> with glints of light. We are the space
> between the fish and the moon,
> while we sit here together.
> —Rumi

When we surf outside reefs, at sunset
We put our feet up on our boards and watch
Each suspicious movement and dark shadow
In the water, until finally the moon
Rises. We convince ourselves we're safe.
Lord only knows what's watching us waiting.

Waves arrive like fast moving solid lines
In moonlight; and for those who've lost their place
In the line-up in the weird light, the price
Is high—a wipe-out in daylight can be
Bad enough, but at night, if a set's first
Wave gets you, your night may well be over.

Waves arrive like fast moving shadows in
Moonlight as the incoming swell traces
hard, dark lines on the gray open water.
When the wave jacks up on the reef, only
The face glows white and the feathering crest
Shines like the plume of some exotic bird.

As we drop in, the waves fold into quick
Hollow curls with deep pockets and slick
Long faces. Water slapping the bottom
Of the board and, behind, the collapsing
Wave is all we hear as we climb and drop
And we know we're on a fast track to Heaven.

DANCING THE WAVES

for Milan Kundera

This dance is the joy of existence.
—Rumi

With the buoyant grace and illumination of oceans,
it really is, you know, unbearably light—life.
You feel it in the motion of water or when
you're happy or at peace with the myriad shapes
and itinerant force of waves that wash across seas
or sweep at the shores, the same way changelessness
and change sweep unpredictably through our lives.

The only words that matter need never be spoken,
unless we choose, otherwise "No," "Yes," and "I
love," we make articulate in eloquent action.

This is how life comes: with the lightness a wave-rider
feels when he turns his board along the smooth shear
face of an overhead wave on a windless day before a storm
and settles back in the curl for the rush toward momentary calm.

Self-definition made unbearably light—a life lived in the ambivalent
dismantling of the moment, the slow roll toward nothing
that makes the paddle out through the waves all the more worthwhile.

"Spinner Dolphins: Hawai'i"

NECESSITY

Best wakefulness in sleep, wealth
in having nothing. . . .

The sky bears its neck so beautifully,
but gets no kiss.
—Rumi

What is necessary we can carry
in both hands at a dead run;
what is unnecessary we cannot carry
at all without the help of others.

But the soul and a kiss square on the face
of the moon or neck of the sky
are weightless and as necessary as air,
yet these we cannot carry at all.

What is necessary we cannot carry
but, like raising a hymn or a hope, carries us.
We become all that we can carry and cannot.
Necessity redeems us, raises us up, bears us away.
"Boats cannot move without water."

TA'I CHI CH'UAN

I slide like an empty boat pulled over water.

In the midst of making form, Love
made this form that melts form. . . .
—Rumi

In the Mo'ili'ili Community Center
Silent Dance Room, Leong Lao Shih
teaches twenty students one-hundred-and-eight forms
—she says we are "playing t'ai chi."

We practice the "Mother Form,"
origin of all forms. We begin with nothing.
Our arms inscribe a circle, like holding a bowl filled
with breath, breath become water. We move as if through water.
Life carved in wide arcs. Do not spill a drop.

Lao Shih says, "Empty your mind;
let it fall like a leaf to rest in your belly. . . .
the lower *tan tien,* the color of a slate gray sea.
Imagine a straight line runs from the center
of the earth through the soles of your feet,
out the top of your head, and connects
directly to the center of Heaven. Imagine
a many-colored dragon rising from the slate-grey sea. . . ."
We try to ignore the heat and, from outside,
street noise and the chatter of T.V.

I.

"Beginning form." Start facing North.
"Raise hands (pull back)." "Strum the Lute (press forward)."
Then "Grasp the Bird's Tail," for the first of many times.
Leong Lao Shih says that in "White Crane Flaps Its Wings,"
We find stillness in motion, emptiness in form.
In transitions we seek balance—the Golden Mean.

Around the lantern-lit yagura in the parking lot
Bon Dancers move in unison to taiko drums and shamisen
Rehearsing the circle-dance they will share with the spirits
Of ancestors returning to the Western Heaven.
We learn "As If Shutting A Door."

In another room of the Community Center,
on a scratched linoleum tile floor, incongruous,
people pale from working in offices practice
putting invisible golf balls into non-existent holes.
(Perhaps more goes on here than meets the eye.)
We practice "Carry Tiger to the Mountain."

II.

We begin Series II with "Fist Under Elbow."
In a side room, the Hawaii Visitors' Bureau
Meets with the Junior Chamber of Commerce to argue
Whether to build a Convention Hall and Visitors Center in the park.
Their voices sharp, intrusive, filled with conviction.
Lao Shih says, "Repulse Monkey,"
And I think to myself, we're all visitors here.

From far away, Lao Shih's voice summons me back,
"Needle at the Bottom of the Sea." I think, "more irony."
"Step forward and Grasp Bird's Tail."
Then the grace of "Cloud Arms" consumes me.

III.

Series III begins with "High Pat the Horse."
A student yelps, breaks from the silent line,
Another sidesteps gingerly, as a cockroach darts across the room,
Cuts left, then right. Leong Lao Shih moves undisturbed
Through the forty-forth form, "Step Back to Form Seven Stars."
We feel foolish and ashamed and having been so easily distracted.

Tonight the Center also hosts classes in cooking
and *Ikebana*. From these rooms we hear laughter,
unlike the rooms where the business men haggle
or the golfers are still intent on their invisible sport.
From somewhere, sounds of a radio float in.

Once someone complained about the noise outside.
Leong Lao Shih smiled, quoted Chuang Tzu:
       "As you float down the river, going your way,
       if your boat is struck by another boat,
       you yell, even swear, at the other boatman.
       You yell only because there is someone there.
       If the other boat is empty, there is no one
       to yell at, no one to hear your anger
       and so you remain silent and continue on.
       The secret to remaining calm, therefore,
       is to empty your own boat as you sail across the world."
Leong Lao Shih laughed, said practice, "Carry Tiger to the Mountain."
Series III ends with "Grasp the Birds' Tail," again, then "Single Whip."

IV.

The transition to Series IV is subtle. Pivot East, "Strum the Lute."
When the termites swarm in summer, geckos
Inside the glowing spheres of Chinese paper lanterns
Shuffle and scratch in a feeding frenzy—in rice-paper
Shades an eerie dance of silhouettes and shadows.
"Jade Girl Works the Shuttle," a mandala in the center of the set,
Then "Clouds Arms" and "Single Whip." Nature goes its way.

V.

In Series V, the twenty move as one. "Snake Creeps Down."
We move in silent unison, each in some interior space.
In the rain forest at the back of Manoa Valley near the foot
Of the falls, a mongoose sleeps in a rock crevice
While rats devour the remnants of a bird's carcass
Or hiker's lunch. "White Crane Spreads Its Wings."

(Lao Shih always says do all 108 forms each morning
at sunrise and again at evening—especially with a full moon rising.)
This morning an unfinished cup of cold coffee stood abandoned
in the sink as I filled a glass with tap water. I glanced down
and was startled by my own face, like the moon,
staring back at me reflected full and round in the stale coffee—
I don't even like coffee, but I like the moon.
We do "Step Up Form Seven Stars"; "Step Back Ride the Tiger."

VI.

In Series VI, the lesson becomes clear:
T'ai Chi is a river, with smooth
flowing places and rough water places—
like the cadences of free verse—

some tumult, some stillness and calm.
"Turn Body—Double Lotus Swing."
The body is the landscape across and through
which the river flows. "Draw Bow and Shoot the Tiger."
Pivot. Slow now, "Step forward and High Pat the Horse."
Gliding, again, "Step forward and Grasp the Bird's Tail."
Settle into "Closing Form." Each muscle, and nerve, and bone relax.
Mind empty but aware, we stand, eyes half-closed— radiant calm.

The river is Chi that always returns to the place of its beginning.
The Soul has become still, while the body is glowing.
Class and Master bow to one another, give silent thanks
and honor the twenty-one rivers that flow here into one Ocean.

"THIS CANDLE DOES NOT BURN;
IT ILLUMINATES"

I said, "But I can't get to You!
You are the whole dark night,
and I am a single candle."
—Rumi

On a table in darkened room
            in a darkened house;
In a darkened world, a candle
            illuminates a rose,
Blooming and fragrant, and "we
Are just strangers who have wandered in."

ENTERING THE UNDERWORLD

Keep walking, though there's no place to get to.
Don't try to see through the distances.
That's not for human beings. Move within,
but don't move the way fear makes you move.

The mystery does not get clearer
by repeating the question. . . .

—Rumi

We come to a point
where we ease ourselves along,
stepping lightly through darkness,
feeling our way by hand and memory.

Some of us, who have no memory,
are down on all fours,
inching along by touch
and instinct, not knowing what
we approach or what approaches us.

When we realize we can stand
and the earth will not fall away
beneath us and there is no matter if it does,
we know at once there's nothing mysterious
and we'll find what we seek in the obvious.

"Manta Ray, Hawai'i"

SUFI ANGER IN THE LATE 20th CENTURY

> I have lived on the lip
> of insanity, wanting to know reasons
> knocking on a door. It opens.
> I've been knocking from the inside.
>   —Rumi

Sometimes it's just too difficult living in a place
where the trees do not have the decency to shed
their leaves and where the birds nest in every season.

So why, especially on a warm night with a batik moon,
full and streaked with cloud, when even the insects are still,
and the ocean at rest laps languidly at every shore,

Why is this night, of all nights, the night you choose
to call me, like a nightmare, offering me a hole to fall into?
Oh, my Soul, or is it fearing your silence, I've called you?

THE SUM OF THINGS

> I honor those who try
> to rid themselves of any lying,
> who empty the self
> and have only clear being there.
> —Rumi

You are a hole in the unnecessary
that makes ground and sky seem necessary.

Whose life are you living?
Whose lines do you speak?
Where did you get them?

This tree, being in itself,
does not need you, and its not
needing you says you do not exist.

When you understand this,
You will begin to vanish, unless
you can make up a new story
about why you are necessary.

THE OPEN SECRET

I am telling you a secret
Do you hear it?

We send messages back and forth
All night. They are in code,
Like water reflecting moonlight.

I am telling you a secret.
Can you hear it?

Rumi says, "Out beyond ideas
Of wrong-doing and right-doing,
There is a field. I will meet you there."

I am telling you a secret.
We are closer to each other than to ourselves,
And the only field is the field we meet in.

I am telling you a secret.
One day, we will all walk empty-handed
Down the same path, through the same door.

I am telling you a secret.
You can read it in the inscription the moon
Leaves on water after the sun has risen.

I am telling you a secret.
God is closer to us than we are to ourselves,
And the only field is the field we meet in.

I am telling you a secret.
There are no secrets, only fields.
I will meet you there.

EYE OF THE STORM

Someone fills the cup in front of us:
We taste only sacredness.

A mouth is not for talking.
A mouth is for tasting this sweetness.
—Rumi

The storm always comes, or the bee sting,
Or the boy throwing rocks, or the anger of another.
"Something opens our wings. Something
makes boredom and hurt disappear."

When the heart aches, the eye still sees.
"Be a lamp, or a lifeboat, or a ladder.
Help someone's soul heal.
Walk out of your house like a shepherd."

It is good to learn to sleep like birds do
With their heads tucked under their wings —
Reposing near the heart beat
But alert to every sound around them.

WHEN IMPENDING DANGER
BREAKS THE CALM

Even the startled birds cry out
       in the panic of darkness
       buffeted by wind,
Like infants asleep or troubled men
       shaken by unwelcome dreams.

"Don't grieve," the Soul says.
"Anything you lose
       comes round in another form."

ELEGY
(Sea Burial)

for John Middleton

> Men and angels speak one language.
> The elusive ones finally meet.
> —Rumi

When the call came from Denver this afternoon that you'd slipped
away in your sleep, I knew a veteran sailor (even
one who loved mountains) could not die so far from the ocean
without passing by a familiar landfall one last time.

So I paddled my numbness and grief out past the breakers
at "Canoes" and "Populars" to "Paradise," where the quick
curl of the wave enfolds you as if (one wave-rider claims)
to spirit you down a primal path, through the gates of heaven.

I hoped to set my grief adrift upon the open sea.
I sat awhile scanning the horizon between Diamond
Head and the setting sun. As I watched the waves sweep in from
the south, turning as they came toward Honolulu Harbor

And "Pearl," I wondered how many times you sailed in on that
very same tide forty years ago, saw the Diamond Head light
and knew you were coming home. Even then, you must have borne
the clarity of vision that would one day capture in

Print a fallen aspen leaf on a bed of pristine snow,
and must have known how each return only prepares the way
for the next departure, and how each sailing forth, finally,
begins the redemption of circling back upon ourselves.

I recall another departure years ago, and in
my mind's eye see the small boy I once was standing in the
driveway waving to you and to my aunt and cousin as
you left for your last tour in these Islands I now call home.

In the odd configurations ours lives become, I sit
here now and scatter grief and regret like ashes amid
the leis and wreaths of countless arrivals and departures.
I glance seaward at passing ships and salute the outgoing tide.

NA KUPUNA O KE KAI

> When the soul first put on the body's shirt,
> the ocean lifted up all its gifts.
> —Rumi

With slow and deliberate ease, they glide
gracefully like giant green sea-turtles,
these graying beach-boys and old-timers who
still paddle out to sea to meet the waves.

With each stroke, aging muscles pull them through
the unresisting water, guide long-board
and man beyond the whitewater into
the line-up for yet one more day of waves.

I imagine the pain, admire the will.
When the wave takes them, and they heave themselves
to their feet, the waves change them, they become
once more as agile as boys. They turn and glide

across the wave's face, climb and drop, then cut
back to meet the curl, cutting back again
to slide into the true line of the wave—
experience reviving sleeping youth.

A tradition part work and part play—each
wave different from every other, but still
a celebration of the familiar.
Late afternoon finds them talking story

about old times and old friends, and teaching
the next generations of waveriders
how to read in the movements of the sea's
bottom the shape and shades of future waves—

learning in their bones from the ocean-floor
today the color of tomorrow's sky.
Elders giving voice to the remembered
sea. They'll reenact this ritual each day,

until their bodies and years release them.
Then one morning, the men they've grown old with,
their families, and the generations they
have taught will do for them one final time

what they can no longer do for themselves.
With slow and deliberate ease, moving
with the grace of green sea-turtles, longboards
and outriggers will carry their ashes

beyond the surfline and into open
water, where their body's shirt will be spread
in the sanctuary of the waves and
their souls restored to the giving sea.

"Green Sea Turtle, East Shore, O'ahu"

PAU HANA KAHALU'U

> We rarely hear the inward music,
> but we're all dancing to it nevertheless. . . .
>   —Rumi

Slack-key without a guitar, with your luau-feet
and Okinawan roots three generations-deep in this soil,
You sit on a sawed-off wooden chair, tilted
Back against the shed your uncles built,
Sipping wine, late on a grey Friday afternoon.

Dense clouds hide the tops of the Ko'olaus
As if the entire sky were too low
For these shear mountains, the valleys dotted
With red ginger, ti plants, banana, and mango
Trees—dark green cliffs streaked by waterfalls.

Music floats up the valley from the radios
Of pick-up trucks parked down at Hygenic Store,
And it's hard to imagine your growing up here,
But the dog curled up by your feet, as if you'd never
Left, says this Windward valley is home.

You sit facing the mountain, where I'd face the sea.
Behind you Kualoa and Chinaman's Hat where last month
The twin-hulls of the Hokule'a touched land
After retracing the path of the Ancients—they navigated
By the stars. Town-side, we see no stars at all.

Each time I leave here with you, heading back to Honolulu
And the workday that never ends, in my bones I hear
Country Comfort singing "Waimanalo Blues" and feel
As though I'm stealing notes from an older song,
Like slack-key without a guitar, *Pau hana*, Kahalu'u.

LAVA VARIATIONS

for Melba Luna

Where your love reaches the core,
earth-heavals and bright irruptions
spew in the air. The Unseen becomes
a spiritual thing, that simple,
love mixing with spirit.
—Rumi

Tonight we drink wine on the lanai, watch
the red Kona sun darken from peach and fire
to magenta, then cool to cobalt flecked with stars.

Our conversation, like the landscape, erupts
with anecdote, metaphor and story. Everywhere
themes, motifs, and memories recapitulate themselves,

New mingles with old. Lights from houses flow down
the mountain; silhouettes of clouds, fishing boats,
and outriggers guard the horizon, await the rising moon.

The mynah spills bits of ripe mango from its beak,
orange pulp rolls across slate-grey patches on
mildewed leaves and down the mottled, ash-like branch.

Tomorrow the lava we've come to watch will cross
the road to meet the incoming tide. Tropes
will seem senseless as out of the steam and molten
glow of smoke, new land forms, oceans boil and deepen.

LETTING GO

Live in the nowhere that you came from,
even though you have an address here.

Show me the way to the ocean!
—Rumi

Birds build nests, raise their young, then fly
Off to build other nests in other times.

Our limitations prevent us
From seeing departures and arrivals

As the same—this especially when
we care. Yet we are not grateful for both

Grief and joy, or disappointment
and desire. We do not celebrate

Suffering or creation, rejoice
Then let them go. We crave affirmation.

We imagine transitions as
Simple feats for others as well as birds,

But for our own dislocations
decry the injustice, speak bitter words.

Each place we nest for a season,
We have chosen as the best in its time.

Dwell there serenely before moving on,
Then visit the sea and embrace the moon.

BODHISATTVA POEM

I need a mouth as wide as the sky
to say the nature of a True Person,
language as large as longing.

Essence is emptiness.
Everything else, accidental.
—Rumi

If I speak today
Or if I speak tomorrow,
        it matters not.

If I go before you
Or if I follow after,
        it matters not.

That I speak or do not
Is all that matters
        or matters not.

If the Buddha creates heaven,
Then he will. If he does not,
        then I will.

There is no reason to create heaven
And there is no reason not to.
        That is why it shall be done.

If I repeat the name of the Buddha ten times,
Then I repeat my own name ten times.
        It is the same thing.

    Amida, Amida, Amida.

DARK WATER

The soul at dawn is like darkened water
that slowly begins to say *Thank you, thank you.*
—Rumi

In early morning and late afternoon
The big waves glide in, bearing down
out of deep shadows on the horizon,
never giving up their darkness.

That is how you come to know them—
by the darkness they never surrender.
Sometimes you just wait for them to arrive,
Othertimes you turn your board and paddle out
To meet them, hoping that's enough.
It's a wonder how the benign dark surge
       can meet the reef and jack-up
       in front of you into a 10-foot
       white-crested wave big enough
       to pull you under and pin you
while the next wave forms and then the next.
Each shadow arrives like an unasked for promise.

When you enter the ocean, you become the ocean's.
At times it holds you gently, at others it won't let you go.
It pulls as if the souls that find life in such dark places
try to hold you back, make a companion of you. Relax.
Deny the impulse to use force against force. Wait. Then
Swim toward the light, when you can;
               but be a friend to darkness, also.

UPANISHAD RESONANT

We've come again to the knee
of that seacoast no ocean can reach.

Tie together all human intellects.
They won't stretch to here.

—Rumi

When I rest,
My folded arm cradles my head,
Just as the curve of the radiant
Land cradles my dancing soul,
Receives my sleeping body.

When I rise,
The outline of my body remains
On this bed, just as the outline
Of my life will remain on the vibrant
Face of the many-colored earth.

When I lie down forever,
"My voice will go into my mind;
my mind into my breath;
my breath into heat;
the heat into the world soul;"
A fine and resonant sleep,
One note in a simple tune.

SURFING THE WORLD-SOUL

> Every *moment,*
> if it is genuinely inside you,
> brings you what you need.
> —Rumi

Sometimes, when you're positioned just right and gliding
      inside the wave's curl, side-slipping through all
      of the innocence there ever was or ever will be,
You feel you could ride forever, dissolve in the unmaking sea.

STILL POINT IN MOTION

> We have fallen into the place
> Where everything is music.
> —Rumi

For just a moment, an age, the off-shore
winds suspend the wave, hold you at the top,
until the swell rises, folds, and lets you
drop into the quick curl for the long slide
across the wave's face where heaven and earth
meet. Your heart stops, breath stops, mind stops, world stops.
Then time and space intersect and stop, but
the soul continues its journey, a still point
in motion—the dance of rider and sea.

"Spinner Dolphins: Kaho'olawe"

Source Works for Rumi Epigraphs

Rumi. *Birdsong*. Coleman Barks, trans. Athens, GA : Maypop. 1993.

_____ *Feeling the Shoulder of the Lion*. Coleman Barks, trans. Vermont: Threshold Books. 1991.

_____ *Like This*. Coleman Barks, trans. Athens, GA : Maypop. 1990.

_____ *One-Handed Basket Weaving*. Coleman Barks, trans. Athens, GA : Maypop. 1991.

_____ *Open Secret: Versions of Rumi*. John Moyne and Coleman Barks, trans. Vermont: Threshold Books. 1984.

_____ *These Branching Moments*. John Moyne and Coleman Barks, trans. Providence: Copper Beech Press. 1988.

_____ *This Longing*. Coleman Barks and John Moyne, trans. Vermont: Threshold Books. 1988.

_____ *Unseen Rain: Quatrains of Rumi*. John Moyne and Coleman Barks, trans. Vermont: Threshold Books. 1986.

OTHER BOOKS BY ANOAI PRESS

The Separating Sickness
By
Ted Gugelyk
Milton Bloombaum
(Published for the Ma'i Ho'oka'awale Foundation)

Mango Lady and Other Stories From Hawaii
By
Ted Gugelyk

Waxing the Lunar Mountain Apple
By
Steven Curry

Two Surf Stories for Children
By
Fred Van Dyke
(2nd edition)

Exiles from Time: Stories of Hawaii
By
Ian MacMillan

ANOAI PRESS publishes literature of all types-novels, short stories, oral history, poetry and children's books. We are particularly interested in Hawaiian-Pacific and East-West themes. Topics of interest to senior surfers are also a specialty.
